Especially for you!
Lourdes Villena Amoloria

~*~

A Kiss From An Angel
~*~

A Kiss From An Angel
~*~

*In loving memory of our beautiful daughter,
Mary Jo Villena Amoloria*

A Kiss From An Angel

Kiss from an Angel
How to Turn Your Grief into A Gift from Heaven

http://kissfromanangel.info/

Copyright © 2014 Lourdes Villena Amoloria All Rights Reserved

No part of this book may be reproduced, stored in a retrieval system or transmitted in any form. Reproduction by electronic, mechanical, photocopying, recording means or otherwise without prior written permission from the publisher, Lourdes Villena Amoloria, is strictly forbidden.

DISCLAIMER

The people and events described and depicted in this book are for educational purposes only. While every attempt has been made to verify that the information provided in this book is correct and up to date, the author assumes no responsibility for any error, inaccuracy or omission.

If advice concerning legal or related matters is needed, the services of a qualified professional should be sought. This book is not intended for use as a source of professional advice.

The tools, stories and information are provided as examples only; not as sources of professional advice.

National Library of Australia Cataloguing-in-Publication entry

Creator:	Amoloria, Lourdes Villena, author.
Title:	Kiss from an Angel : How to Turn Your Grief into a Gift from Heaven
ISBN:	978-0-9941885-1-9 (paperback)
	978-0-9941885-0-2 [ebk]
Subjects:	Amoloria, Lourdes Villena
	Mothers—Biography
	Infants--Death--Psychological aspect
	Bereavement--Psychological aspects
	Parental grief
	Mental healing.
Dewey Number	Dewey Number: 155.9370852

A Kiss From An Angel
~*~

Dedication

I dedicate this book to my husband Joe who has been my unfailing source of strength, love, support and inspiration on this journey. I also dedicate this book to four beautiful angels, taken to grow up in heaven, Mary Jo, her sister Theresa Rose, cousins Claire Anne and Maria Theresa. They are forever loved, never forgotten just as all our loved ones who have also departed and taken a piece of our hearts to heaven.

I also dedicate this book to all my family members, friends, educators, mentors and all the wonderful human angels who are proactive in their love and compassion for others. Those who are not afraid to help one another or to share their knowledge, skills, time and comfort so that another human being can be inspired to take another breath filled with hope knowing that all challenges in life are temporary. That against all odds, love, inherent goodness in humankind and your unwavering belief in God and your faith in will always prevail.

Lastly, I dedicate this book to anyone who is still grieving. I sincerely believe you too will one day receive the great gift grief can give. To know how much love we are capable of and that death is not an end to love, but a catalyst to making sure you are living life to the fullest knowing how limited sometimes our time can be with our loved ones.

With unending gratitude, love and hope,

Lourdes Villena Amoloria

CONTENTS

Foreword 11

Introduction 15

Too Much Love Too Little Time 21

Happiness Beyond Limits 37

Hell On Earth 59

Almost Magical Synchronicity in Abundance 77

Application of Theories on Grieving 103

Transforming Grief into Gifts 117

Messages of Love for Mary Jo 123

About the Author 145

Today will never come again,
Be a blessing,
Be a friend,
Encourage someone,
Take time to care,
Let your words heal and not wound.

Anonymous

Foreword

Kind words can be short and easy to speak, but their echoes are truly endless. **Mother Teresa**

~*~

One can never imagine, in their darkest of thoughts, or their saddest moments, what it would feel like to lose your child. A child that has grown inside your heart, your dreams, your soul and your every waking breath from the moment of conception.

When I heard of Lourdes & Joe's heartfelt story, as a mother of an only child myself, I grieved for their loss deeply. Having to hear any mother or parent relive the pain of losing the unconditional love of their only child, taken from them far too soon, was heart wrenching beyond words.

But in that moment, I also saw the gift of love that Mary Jo, in her short life, had given so generously to the lives of many.

I knew in my heart that it was time for Lourdes and Joe to open the doors of their grief and set it free. And what better way to do that than by sharing her amazing story in a book.

Mary Jo, without a doubt, was a gift from heaven. A kiss from an angel with so much love to give to so many in her short lifetime, and boy did she touch many people's hearts as you will read in Chapter 7. It was an amazing journey that needed to be honoured, celebrated and remembered with happiness, joy and love, forever.

That is why it was so important for Lourdes to write this book in loving memory of her child Mary Jo.

Every child in the world is a gift from God no matter how long or short their time on earth. They are here to spread laughter, joy and unconditional love to every person they come in contact with. And the biggest gift that Lourdes and Joe could give to their beautiful little girl is to allow her loving smile to continue to heal the grieving hearts of others all around the world.

It has taken Lourdes and Joe 20 long years to set their

Foreword

~*~

heart free from the grief and loss of their only child and I am so proud to be able to help them turn their story 'A Kiss From An Angel' into the beautiful Gift From Heaven that she is to this day.

In this heartfelt story you will laugh, you will shed a tear and you may even get a little upset and angry along the way. But the message is clear.....it is better to have had the gift of life and love, then to never have been Kissed From An Angel at all.

For those of you who read this beautiful story, I hope it brings you peace and comfort in the knowing that your loved ones are with you always and even though they may have left this earth, they never really leave your heart and soul.

Mary Jo, I know you have been with your mother and father every step of the way. And that you were the ink behind the pen that wrote these words and the water behind the tears of love that have been shed with each passing memory.

This beautiful book is a gift to you from earth, from

two people who love you very, very much and who want to share your unconditional love within these pages, so that others can find the strength within to turn their own grief into a beautiful gift from heaven.

Enjoy this amazing story A Kiss from An Angel.

With love always

Pam Brossman, 10 Times #1 Amazon Best Selling Author CEO, Pam Brossman.com

Introduction

A Kiss from an Angel
~*~

Grieving is a complicated response over the loss of someones much valued presence in your life. Often the loss of a loved one because of death can bring suffering no words can ever describe. The psychic wound is so deep, every cell of your system is affected, and there is no place to hide or a way to bury the inner longing for the physical presence of the deceased.

This book brings out in the open the bereaved parents experience of joy and fulfilment during the birth of a much wanted and only child, Mary Jo, the gift of parenthood, the unexpected condition of their baby, the triumph of raising her against medical odds, the drama of her life and death and how her parents found the gift amidst grief, loss and tears and the consuming grip on one's psyche because of multiple losses.

There is an unexplained synchronicity in our lives that connects us all. Call it divine guidance, the Universal Mind, sometimes we cannot really explain but then we see magical day-to-day coincidences, events and strangers drawn into our lives like magnets and magical things happen. Are they really miracles or the pre-programming of our real purpose in life? Like the idea of writing of this book, the author kept the tears within herself for more than eighteen years only to realize that sharing one's experience of grief and loss is the right path to connect and feel the wounds in our psyche so they can be out in the open and together we can heal. Wonderful human angels appeared, guiding her to unearth what was hidden, what needed to be shared and to be written to help in the healing of others too. What a wonderful realization that like-minded human beings are all part of this multidimensional universe being guided so we can help one another and be inspired to walk our own destiny with faith.

This book is for the strong and the lucky ones who

Introduction

have battled life's challenges with outcomes in a time frame they wanted, this is also for the many, like the author, who hide their broken hearts being busy with a job and other things and just hoping one day the sadness will evaporate into thin air. It is also for anyone who wants to be empowered, to recover and to understand what clinicians and the author actually experienced in facing life's most challenging battle, losing a significant and loved person.

The impact of Mary Jo's death was so unexpected. She was a well-loved child, so well cared for. Why of the many children on planet earth, would she be chosen to die at age of two years and five months despite modern medical facilities? Why were the doctors so blind and deaf to her mother's pleadings for proper medical care? Why were the symptoms ignored? Why should her parents and love ones live with the never-ending possibility that she could have lived if only the medical experts had acted from the space of a truly loving and caring heart rather from just the sterilized medical procedures? So many questions had remained unanswered and perhaps will never be known in her parents' lifetime.

After Mary Jo was buried, her parents were affected with complicated grief from not only her loss but also the futility of fighting the legal system. To say, they were devastated physically, emotionally, behaviorally, psychologically is an understatement. Lourdes, her mother had wished she could have died in her daughter's place. Her father Joe had changed from someone with a generally happy disposition to a person deeply affected with distress. Their lives had changed so dramatically, spiraling to depths of despair, even their faith was in tatters. They were inconsolable; life had lost its meaning.

From the extraordinary anguish of grief and loss, Mary Jo started to appear in her parents' dreams, to other family members, and their circle of friends and even medical people who attended to her. Coincidences beyond the logic of science and practical day-to-day life emerged. Yes, Mary Jo was physically dead, her young and beautiful body buried but her

Introduction

loving and caring spirit came to life and touched her parents and love ones. This book will touch your heart and soul like no other book on grief can. Read every chapter, every page as the reality of so much love and so little time can grip your heart. Learn from her loved ones first-hand experience, the resilience of the human spirit and of divinity intertwined because a little angel named Mary Jo continues to kiss her love ones and so hopefully the readers of this book will also receive the kisses and the gift too.

*Humbleness, forgiveness and love
are the dynamics of freedom.
They are the foundations
of authentic power.*
Gary Zukav

Too Much Love Too Little Time

There are only two ways to live your life. One is as though nothing is a miracle. The other is as though everything is a miracle. **Albert Einstein**

~*~

"Please, please do not take my grief away." To this day, this is still the pleading of our broken hearts, a pleading to anyone who would suggest we completely let go of our grief over the loss of our only child, Mary Jo. The intensity of this plea has altered through the years since 3rd of April, 1996 when Mary Jo died and earned her angel wings. This appeal, not to take our grief away, is not easy to understand especially by people who have not experienced significant loss in their lives. Incongruous as it may seem, to some grievers missing the departed dead, isolating oneself and feeling sad is a way of connecting with the departed person. Taking away grief to some people is like forgetting the dead person; hence, many people learn to live with grief after the death of a loved one. Grief can shake our whole being like the fiercest storm that can uproot the strongest tree and yet the same experience can also strengthen our resolve to make a commitment to live life fully, knowing we do not have much time to share the love we can give to each other. No words can take away the grief of having so much love to share and yet the preferred recipient of that love is no longer able to feel it physically. They can no longer feel the warmth of our hugs and kisses. The sparkling, beautiful and expressive eyes are closed forever. Grief is more than just the absence of the physical person. After the death of a child, comes the emptiness of being in a home that was once so full of laughter and happiness. The crib is empty; all around the room are reminders of the wonder of having a young life in our care. Even the dolls seem to have died, the temperature of the room has gone cold, and I feel I am going mad. In reality, the body must be undergoing so many physiological and emotional changes in response to the intense grief, hence the myriad of symptoms like headaches, insomnia, anxiety, depression, lack of self-confidence, and loss of appetite, heart palpitations and other symptoms at different times and stages of grief. Some people after a period of time are able to ride off the symptoms and elevate themselves to a certain level of spiritual awareness and acceptance. There are some grievers however, who resort to taking drugs, alcohol and other maladaptive behaviours to mask and take away the pain. Research shows many can recover with professional help, support of family and friends but often it is the individual who decides what to do to continue to live a meaningful life despite the grief and irreplaceable loss. Death also means the loss of so many dreams of being together in life's journey. Someone's grief may trigger a response in us; it awakens us to the grim possibility of what can happen if we are in the place of that person who has just lost a child, parents, siblings or other much-loved person. Grief can illicit different emotional and physical symptoms as well as social and spiritual outlooks in people of different culture, religions and upbringing. One thing however can link us all, the very human feeling of sadness and yearning and also the indomitable spirit that makes us rise above the challenges of grief and loss.

There are days like birthdays, anniversaries, Christmas, family reunions or just a whisper of a song, a little reminder and the triggers of pain can surface with an intensity and magnitude that can be overwhelming. Many times, I felt my whole being drowned in misery and emotional paralysis due to the intense pain of losing a much wanted and well-loved only child.

Joe and I come from very close-knit families and the birth of a new family member is always a joyous occasion. When we went home with Mary Jo for the first and last time in 1995, family members on both sides were deeply touched by Mary Jo's presence as Mary Jo warmed to them as if she had known them all her life. Mary Jo can be choosy with new acquaintances and what a delight to see her clap her hands and keep on smiling to family members she had just met. I am now convinced memory is not only stored in our conscious mind, but also even in the blood that flows through all of us, and the psychic field and energy that binds family together; all these link loved ones in ways beyond explanation. Everyone was vying for her attention and she was so delighted to be the centre of attention. We went home in March 1995 for the funeral of my father. We never thought that a year later, it was Mary Jo's turn to die. After her death we were so focused on our grief in Sydney, that we were oblivious to the grief of Mary Jo's grandmother, my own mother, her uncles and aunties and their families, the care givers and some medical staff and other people and children who had known Mary Jo. One of her playmates, John Aaron, had asked me, "Why Mary Jo should die and be buried under the ground." I answered the proverbial reply to ease the pain of a child, "Mary Jo is no longer under the ground she is in heaven." To this, he almost cried and looked at the grave more intently, "I don't want her in heaven, I want her here."

I never really understood much about grief before but our child's death changed all that. We have become more compassionate and understanding when someone else is going through the rawness of emotions associated with grief and loss. Every person grieves differently. Some people can let go of grief in less than a month, perhaps a year but with some chronic grievers, the freshness of grief can be triggered anytime and lasts for many, many years even a lifetime.

Losing anything of value be it a small or a significant loss triggers many different emotions. Some people handle their emotions well, other people, like me, experience grief somewhat like a roller coaster ride, ups and downs and sometimes not knowing when to stop. Why some people hold on to, or unable to recover from the pain of losing a love one, the loss of a relationship, loss of a job, loss of dreams and opportunities and other life incidents involving loss is definitely not an easy question to answer. In my case, I can honestly say I was totally unprepared to handle the emotions associated with losing a much wanted, well-loved only child. I use to take pride in being a person who could control anger and easily forgive and move on but this side of myself changed when our only child died. The feelings of being aggressively angry because there was nothing I could do in extending our daughter's life, the anger associated with helplessness and venting out to the medical and legal system had created havoc on my physical and emotional wellbeing.

3rd of April, 1996, Wednesday of the Christian calendar's Holy Week was the date I wished was forever wiped out of the world's calendar. Mary Jo, our only child was confirmed dead by a tearful nurse who just looked at me and nodded with tears in her

A Kiss From An Angel

~*~

eyes, there was no need for words. For thirteen days and nights, we had our eyes glued on the various monitoring screens that had endless tubes, needles, connections attached to our dying child. I had asked the intensive care nurses what some of the data was for and I learned that the most vital signs are on oxygen saturation level, the heart and brain monitors. The alarm sounds had kept us close to nervous breakdowns as it meant our daughter being so close to death. Finally, when I saw the flat lines, I was unprepared for the depths of sorrow that had enveloped me. Joe, my husband gave a big cry as he embraced the lifeless body of Mary Jo. I stood frozen, immersed on the scene unfolding in front of my eyes, the two most important people in my life in a scene so surreal. My mind was so numb. I wish I could have died instead, so I couldn't witness my husband's grief watching as the life was slipping from his beautiful Mary Jo.

The nurse pulled the curtains around Mary Jo's bed. We had been in the intensive care for nearly two weeks since our daughter was admitted to the Children's hospital. It all started with flu like symptoms. Knowing how fragile toddlers can be, we had taken her to our family doctor who diagnosed her symptoms as a viral infection with no need for antibiotics. He prescribed an over the counter prescription in case fever developed. Unconvinced, Joe and I took her again to the same general practitioner and after a physical exam and temperature check, he said he could not see anything serious and assured us she will be fine in a few days' time. My instinct was not in harmony with what the doctor was saying hence I requested for a specialist to see her and again nothing serious was detected.

Mary Jo was sleeping most of the day and I was starting to be really worried as she was a playful, smiling, good-natured child. One afternoon, I told Joe if doctors could not find anything wrong with her we might as well admit her to the hospital as she was not her usual self. When we went to the hospital, we had to wait a long time as Mary Jo was not considered an emergency case. They took some tests and sent us home. I could not stand another night not knowing what the tests results can be so Joe and I bundled Mary Jo up and went back to the hospital literally begging for admission.

We had top of the line private family health fund cover to make sure we were prepared for our daughter's medical needs. Shortly after, when the hospital finally decided to admit Mary Jo, she was re-examined and intravenous fluids were administered. The doctor could hardly find a vein in her plump wrist; my heart ached hearing her cries.

The two years and four months that Mary Jo was with us, were the most remarkable years of our lives. Mary Jo was so wanted, so well loved and despite the challenges of being premature, with Down's syndrome and breach, Mary Jo was a fighter. She survived the difficult birthing conditions, the challenges of being a special child with special needs. We were so lucky to be given so much support helping us take care of Mary Jo.

She had intervention medically, occupational therapists regularly visited and monitored her progress, and a speech therapist was also helping her develop language skills. With hawk eye vigilance we followed all medical suggestions and intervention plans for her physical and mental development. It was so rewarding to see her personal health record improve as time goes by. Nonetheless, despite all the care given to her she had occasional bouts of flu, was hospitalized for bronchitis when she was only three months old and had her adenoids surgery in February, 1996. We never thought that pneumonia would take her life as we had done everything possible to ensure her good health.

Loving and caring for Mary Jo made a lot of difference in her physical and cognitive development. She was full of life, always smiling, always wanting to please us with her karate kicks, showering us with many hugs and kisses. She was a born kisser, always wanting to kiss everyone she liked. Perhaps instinctively she already knew she was only on earth for a short while. Mary Jo was a very sociable toddler, always happy to be the centre of attention at home and in public places. It was very hard for us to accept that my husband and I will grow old without our only child. Our dreams to see her grow, to be engaged, to marry and give us grand children went up like a puff of smoke the day she died.

It took a while for reality to sink in. Before I had Mary Jo I was a self-confident corporate person, well trained in marketing and sales and I had risen to higher levels in the multinational company I was working for. Motherhood made me humble enough to forego any dreams to become more successful in the corporate world and having a child was worth giving up my career dreams for. Then, so unexpectedly, life has different cycles for us to live through.

Looking back, the love we had for Mary Jo also strengthened the love my husband and I had for each other. We knew no one else in this world knew the depths of our pain so we tried hard to support each other. We always felt Mary Jo was there making sure her parents remained united and devoted to each other. We were well supported by sincere friends and family during our times of intense grief and to this day, these kind friends have never left us. They were never too busy to listen to our grieving hearts or dismiss our need to keep recalling Mary Jo's beautiful moments, many of which they were a part of too. No one deserves to grieve alone. While we do the grieving, friends, family and support groups can help ease the pain. It is understandable if we feel all alone, as if no one else can understand what we are going through but it is better not to cut ourselves off from the stream of life.

As the reader takes the journey of knowing Mary Jo's story, it is my intention to make the person aware that while there is an intensity of losing, recovery is also possible. A well-meaning friend once asked whether given the choice, if it would be better to be a mother and lose a child or never to be a mother at all and be spared the grief.

It is a tough question to answer, but I told her that the

joy of being a mother and having a relationship with my child and husband, being a complete family is an experience I will always treasure. Some parents separate, go into drugs, alcohol and other addictions, or lose the desire to be in tune with life again. Death affects us all differently, whether the loss of a husband who was our provider or a mother caring for her children, the roles we had are changed. Children who lose a parent can become vulnerable and defenseless. Loneliness can cause people who lose a much-loved spouse, to get into the dating game to find a replacement, some get lucky and get a better partner, and others get victimized. For most people the first three months after the death of a significant loved one is the most trying time. We were so lucky we had supportive family and friends that helped us weather the brunt of grief but even then, the emotional and psychological scars have left a stinging intrusion in our hearts and souls.

Sometimes we long for the days that will never come back again, irrational as it is, but the mind and emotions cannot just switch off the memories of a precious love one. How true is the expression though, that it better to have loved and lost than never to have loved at all. While we still have the time, and while we and our loved ones are still alive, love is the most powerful, life-sustaining gift we can give to each other. As this book progresses, the reader will vicariously experience what really happened to our child and though extremely painful and still questionable, rest assured that there is life after the death of a most precious child and it can be a truly meaningful life, dedicated to the living and in the service of others, regardless of age.

*"To Love and win is the best thing.
To love and lose, the next best thing".*

William M. Thackeray

Happiness Beyond Limits

It is better to light a candle than to curse the darkness.
Chinese Proverb
~*~

"You are pregnant," Joe announced without a shred of doubt. That was in April of 1993, one beautiful evening after dinner. I was relaxing in the lounge room and he was coming out from the kitchen. I remember well and with amazing clarity the expression on his face, so filled with loving concern and absolute certainty. To say I was euphoric, enraptured and terribly excited is an understatement. Words cannot express how I felt.

My periods had always been irregular so I did not

expect to be pregnant. I was turning 40 in two months and to expect a baby was pure bliss. I have always dreamt of becoming a mother. I felt colour rush to my face, as a warm deliciousness spread through my body, the feeling of excitement was overwhelming. I did not doubt Joe's announcement as he is by nature a very intuitive person and his premonitions are always accurate.

The next day, I visited our GP, had a pregnancy test and he confirmed I was pregnant. My pregnancy was stress free and I was lucky not to experience morning sickness at all. My health condition was excellent so I decided to continue with my job as administrative assistant. Both my general practitioner and obstetrician recommended amniocentesis, a medical test that takes a sample of amniotic fluid so the laboratory can check on the chromosomes of the baby. The test can rule out some possible birth defects like Down syndrome and many others. When I was informed that the procedure can be invasive and have a minor risk of miscarriage Joe and I did not see the logic of undergoing the test as we were determined to keep our baby no matter what possible birth defects he or she is born with. The prospect of being parents placed both of us in auto mode for happiness almost all of the time, we were literally over the moon. We started bonding with our child even before she was born. I had worked with a firm that manufactured baby's formula and so we had exposure to the latest medical findings on fetal development and health. Part of my job description had been to help organize medical seminars and clinical meetings for medical personnel. I had always been interested in the studies relating to the development of the brain, pre-natal health of both mother and baby, infant nutrition and more. I had also made friends in the medical, pharmaceutical, marketing, and sales community, and had developed precious friendships with co-employees, especially Raquel, Joe's sister, my best friend and sister in law. Everything seemed pre-programmed for me in becoming a mother, and with the tremendous support and involvement of my husband Joe, it ensured a stress free pregnancy. I felt so privileged to be feeling prepared emotionally, mentally and physically and I loved being pregnant. If there was any discomfort, I was oblivious to the symptoms. There is no price tag for happiness and being a wife and as an expectant mother was a phase of unlimited happiness in my life cycle.

I recalled with fondness how my own mother tackled her pregnancies. I am the eldest in the family and have seven younger brothers and one sister. As a young child, I saw each sibling being added to our family. When I was about six years old, I was convinced that it was my father who gave birth to me. I saw my mother's tummy grow big and every time a baby came, it was a boy, six times in fact, because of my brothers Adriano, Bonnie, Peter, Gerry, Bernard and Joey. My six-year-old mind then made the conclusion that mothers give birth to baby boys and a baby girl only comes from her father. I recall the many times I would cry because our household staff, maids, caretakers and employees in my father's car repair and battery charging business would take turns to tease me because of my belief that my father became pregnant with me. The misconception finally came to an end when my only sister Muffet was born. By then I was around ten years old, already learning some science in school including some of life's lessons on the birds and the bees and everything else my mind could absorb. When my youngest brother, Michael was born, I had totally laughed off my belief about who brought me into this world.

My friends and office mates were quick to notice that I was forever smiling. Every day of my pregnancy was a blessing of happiness beyond measure. Before retiring in the evening, Joe would rub coconut oil on my growing tummy, the pleasurable feeling so intense, a feeling I still recall with fondness. I am sure our baby must have felt the overwhelming love. Ironically, it was Joe who was feeling somewhat nauseous at times. I did not suffer from morning sickness at all but Joe did. Lucky me, while I carried the baby, it was Joe who was feeling the downside of being pregnant. Doctors reading this might know the answer why, sympathetic pregnancy or something else. Sometimes I wished I had experienced morning sickness as that was the only thing missing during my pregnancy that I had so often heard about. Joe did not mind the morning sickness bouts though, as all he wanted was for me to be having a pleasant time as a pregnant woman. Throughout my pregnancy, I often caught myself smiling for no reason. Many strangers smiled back because I smiled at everyone.

Before we were married, Joe had worked as a merchant marine, living overseas since he was a teenager. He had been a well-travelled seaman and eventually settled in Sydney. In 1986, Joe went home and we met for the first time. It was much later in August of 1991 when we finally got married. After we got married, Joe recalled that when he signed our marriage certificate, he remembered that my name Lourdes hit him like a thunderbolt. For many years, he was off and on with various unsuccessful relationships and he recalled kneeling before the image of the Blessed Virgin Mary and begging for a good wife. I had also prayed a novena to St Joseph, the foster father of Jesus that he would intercede for me to have a good husband. Naming our baby then after the Blessed Mother, Mary and St Joseph was an acknowledgment of answered prayers. When Joe and I started to plan names for our baby we chose Mary Jo if she was a girl and Jose Marie if it was a boy.

I did not really know what I was looking for in a man before we got married. All I knew was I just wanted to be married once I was ready to take the plunge. One of the most remarkable conversations I had with my late father was in 1991. I asked him what I would look for in a man if I was to get married. Wisely, he said, observe how your prospective groom deals with his mother, sisters and women who are much less in social standing than him because such behaviour will tell you what kind of man he will be if you choose him to be your husband. Joe topped the assessment as his sisters had always told me how caring he was with them and how close he was with his own mother, Socorro who died of cancer when he was only sixteen years old.

Joe and I had met late in life and falling in love was so unexpected. I was in the Philippines then and all the while Joe was living in Sydney. His sister Raquel is my best friend and we both worked in a pharmaceutical and nutritional company. Our homes were also located in the same suburb in the Philippines. Most members of our immediate household knew each other well except for Joe who was overseas and was already an Australian citizen. Their father Jose was a good friend of my father, Adriano. Later, I learned from my mother's brother, Uncle Milan that Joe and Raquel's father was a fellow war veteran who was their much valued intelligence officer during World War II. Knowing that my own father and maternal Uncle, and father in law were no strangers to each other felt so good. I also felt relieved, as I was not marrying a stranger from overseas after all. In our Filipino culture, close family ties and similarity of

Happiness Beyond Limits

faith mean a lot, not only as a plus factor to help make marriages rock solid but also from a practical point of view. Families often look after each other and when there is harmony with in-laws, there are unlimited potential benefits in terms of emotional, financial, and psychological support. Problems are inevitable but our respective families always managed to retain our identity as a clan, each family member, whether new, old, or departed were considered priceless and forever a member no matter which part of the globe we lived in. Every newborn is always considered a priceless blessing in our families, a strong signal from heaven our family will continue.

Mary Jo's birth was definitely a much-welcomed event. Despite the dramas surrounding her breach delivery, her being diagnosed as a Down syndrome baby, our optimism for her to live a full life was beyond limits. There were so many good things going for her. Physically, she did not look like a typical mongoloid baby. Her features resembled more of a Chinese doll, her full lips and cheeky smiles, dark brown eyes, healthy reddish tan and straight black hair made her look so different but so cute when she is among Caucasian children. Mary Jo was always well dressed. Her aunt, Raquel, always sent her beautiful clothes from America, our friends in Sydney filled her closet with clothes, a supply sufficient until she was seven. Everyone we knew came with gifts of shoes, toys, dolls and so much baby stuff. What tremendous joy it was to dress her up in matching outfits. I felt as though I had a living, precious doll, a beautiful princess and angel entrusted in my care. I never knew motherhood could be this beautiful. Mary Jo had encapsulated our whole being, my husband and I felt so blessed heaven had given us this vulnerable and charming child. Little did we realize she would be with us physically for only two years and four months, but her legacy of love in its purest sense had penetrated every cell in our body, every good thought that crosses our mind. Her influence ignites our hearts to do well to others as we know she continue to guide, protect and love us and has a unique way of connecting us to likeminded people.

In my mind, I had pictured myself being a mother to a debutante, a graduate, the mother of the bride and a proud grandmother. My imagination had run wild with the prospect of seeing our only child go through the process of going to school, meeting new friends, coping with the challenges of being a teenager, then finishing school and ultimately becoming a mother herself and having a good and caring husband like her Papa. Every day, I prayed for her good health, safety and wellbeing. Motherhood is indeed the most remarkable role a woman can have. I had immersed myself in the role, without any hesitation, like fish swimming back to the ocean; I realized that the role I had as a successful corporate woman paled in comparison to the role of being a wife and mother. My heart had expanded to unlimited levels of loving, caring and nurturing this beautiful angel who had been given this chance to be a human being, with my flesh and blood so intertwined in her physical self. Since Mary Jo was born, the gratitude I felt had overwhelmed my body, heart, soul and mind. Every day, I asked God to take care of our only child. Oh how angry, how disillusioned I was when He allowed Mary Jo to die. Years later, it dawned on me that God had complied with my request. He preferred Mary Jo to grow up in heaven with Him, the angels and saints mentoring our dearest daughter so her parents on earth can fulfil the mission He had prepared us for.

There are so many beautiful memories of Mary Jo. One evening, her Papa and I were watching a television program, our eyes glued to the TV set, so we did not notice her crawling around. Suddenly the TV shut down and there she was, clutching the electrical cord she had pulled out from the socket, she laughed to her heart's delight, so amused that our attention was finally focused on her. Mary Jo always surprised us with her cheeky ways. One night, Joe was rocking her to sleep. I saw her eyes closed, her face that of a sleeping angel so incapable of doing anything wrong. Out of nowhere, Joe gave a big wail and almost dropped her. With her sleepy head safely tucked in the crook of his arm, her left hand had made its way to a fleshy part of Joe's back, where she pinched him; an impish grin on her face, her eyes still closed pretending to be asleep. Since then, Joe made sure he cut her fingernails really short and did not force her to sleep.

There were also unexplained things that had happened. One afternoon, we peeped in to see how she was progressing with her afternoon nap. To our surprise, she was standing at the end of her crib looking towards the direction of the altar in the room and she was having an animated conversation as if talking to someone. We slowly entered the room, careful not to disturb her conversation. It was all baby talk and in a language we could not even understand. She was laughing in between syllables. While her hands gripped on the corner of the crib, her eyes were glued to the altar and it seemed to us that she was communicating with someone. We looked where her eyes were focused and were surprised that it was focusing on a statue "the child Jesus of Prague".

Joe and I looked at each other in disbelief, we decided not to stop her from her imaginary conversation but now I know how limited our human vision is, for surely Mary Jo was conversing with someone only her pure and innocent spirit was privileged to see and interact with.

Mary Jo was a cheeky child, who loved attention and was wise to the ways and means to get the attention she wanted. She was less than two years old, but wise enough to realize her parents can get glued to a TV program. She had already seen the connection of the TV plug and the socket hence that one unguarded moment when she crawled to unplug the TV and laughed in victory when Joe and I were surprised the TV screen went blank. On another occasion, when we had put a furniture barricade near the socket to prevent her from electrical accidents, she must have felt a wanting of attention again because we could not find the remote control. We felt her watching us, the look on her face instinctively telling me she knew where the remote control was. She had seated herself in between the lounge seats and when I searched in between the seats, there was the remote control under her. I told this incident to my mother. A few years after Mary Jo's death, my Mom was desperately looking for her glasses and no one could find them inside the house. She remembered Mary Jo's cheekiness in hiding things to get her parents attention so she asked in a loud voice, with full belief her dead grandchild was with her that day, where her glasses were. From the corner of her room, she clearly heard a child's laughter, she went to check the source of the laughter, as she knew there was not any child in the house, and was amazed to find her missing glasses. Now my mother is 84 years old and she feels her memory and cognitive function have wavered, however she continues to claim her grandchild helps her find missing objects if she calls her.

Mary Jo was more outgoing than most of the two year olds I knew then. One time we were attending mass, and as always, it was her father who was holding her when we were in a public place. Mary Jo was looking at the pew behind where we were seated, smiling at some old ladies. Unexpectedly, I saw her raise her right fist ready to punch the old lady's face, quickly Joe tapped her fist but then with one swift swing, she raised her right leg to do a karate round house kick. I could not contain my embarrassment and of course my amusement. Mary Jo was so used to getting attention and making people happy; I bet she could not stand those grumpy faces of the ladies trying to stay focused on the mass. One Sunday, at church again, the only seat was the one near the church choir. Mary Jo always loved music. When I was pregnant, I would listen to music knowing that hearing was the first sense to be developed. The choir was composed mostly of young teenagers singing in perfect harmony, the beats of the music so well blended one could not help but appreciate the talents of these young singers and how they blended their voice to create a heavenly atmosphere. Momentarily, I closed my eyes to immerse myself in the beautiful feeling of being with my loving family, grateful to the almighty God who gave me this priceless gift, to be in the beautiful church where Mary Jo was baptized, the atmosphere of being with fellow worshippers and feeling as though the angelic choir had visited us through the voices of these young singers. Then I heard the voices out of unison, murmurs of uncontrolled laughter coming from the choir members and when I opened my eyes, I saw Mary Jo following the actions of the choir leader. She was raising her hands, her eyes focused on the choir members as if leading the choir. I could not help but laugh myself, as we could not stop her from leading the choir in her very cute and focused way. That day the priest had a very lengthy homily. The church was so quiet, either everyone was listening carefully, or had fallen asleep. After the sermon, Mary Jo made her presence felt, she gave a long sound of intense relief...."yeah." Her voice broke the silence and elicited chuckles from the amused audience. Now every time I am in church, I remember Mary Jo's funny tricks when she was still with us, the memories though poignant, now make me grateful I had personally experienced the joys of having a precocious two year old.

Children must be born linguists, the capacity to understand various languages and even speak it. When Mary Jo was alive, we lived in an apartment block with neighbours of different cultures. Our common area was the grounds where we hung our laundry to dry and we often had a chance to catch up there. In the building were people from the Middle East, Asia, Europeans and Australians. Mary Jo was the only baby in the whole building, and almost everyone had a soft spot for her. Mary Jo had the ability to glue us happily as neighbours, a hallmark of her remarkable personality. She laughs with glee to see the same sex couple across the hall and, despite the war between Iraq and Iran at that time, the Iraqi lady was planting a kiss on Mary Jo's left cheek while the Iranian lady was kissing her right and she was clapping her hands as if in great approval. The masculine somewhat aloof New Zealander is often caught off guard when Mary Jo smiles at him. Another Indonesian lady often comes up to bring her biscuits and some goodies while a Vietnamese refugee who lives in the same building will go out of her way to bring Mary Jo beautiful dresses. The Aussie retired nurse always checks on how Mary Jo was. Mary Jo's language was the language of the heart, no sound, yet so effective in bringing out the hidden love and caring that was so inherent in all who met her. Another proof of her efficiency in communicating was her interaction with an elderly Russian lady who could not speak a word of English. We invited her for tea and Mary Jo immediately reached out to touch her plump, pinkish cheeks. The old lady started to speak to Mary Jo in Russian, Mary Jo responded in syllables we could not understand, they carried on their conversation with laughter in between, I wish I had a movie recorder then, to prove our daughter could understand and speak in Russian. The Russian lady's family knew where to look for her when she went missing, she would be keeping me and Mary Jo company, perhaps teaching Mary Jo to speak better Russian. One day the family left the building. For months we did not see the old lady then one afternoon we opened to a knock on the door to find the old lady wanting to visit her friend. We let her in and immediately they started their animated exchange. Their friendly catch up must have lasted more than two hours, and then came a loud knock on our door; it was the old lady's family. How relieved they were to find her as they said she left their place without permission, they had gone almost crazy looking for her before realizing she must have walked up to our building to see Mary Jo. How right they were.

Another time, we were inside a chemist and saw a Japanese lady waiting for her turn to be served. Mary Jo flashed her smile and the Japanese lady was drawn to Mary Jo like a magnet. She must have said hello or something and I heard Mary Jo respond in what sounded like Japanese. They carried on an exchange for a while, before the Japanese lady said to me, "you have taught your daughter to speak good Japanese." I could not say a word, it was a good thing the chemist called for her to be served, and otherwise she would have been as confused as I was how a two year old without any Japanese heritage could speak to her in her language. Looking back now, it makes a lot of sense, Mary Jo was a living angel who spoke the universal language of loving and caring, speaking the particular language with ease to anyone she met. This is the kind of happiness that fires my heart to this day, a kind of happiness beyond any measure or limitation, a message so badly needed by our world, weary of war and greed.

"The generosity of your time is the most valuable gift you can give."

Sarah Henderson

Hell On Earth

May you live all the days of your life. **Jonathan Swift.**
~*~

Many grieving parents have asked the question, "Why do we have to bury our own children, why not our children burying us in our old age?" No one can really answer this question but we all know life is like a game, sometimes we win, and sometimes we lose. No matter what happens, change in life is inevitable and life does not wait for anyone, it is always moving on. Whether the changes are to our liking or not, they continue and the challenge is to continue living despite the changes of people around us, the environment or even within our own selves be it emotional, physical, psychological or spiritual.

There is no quick fix for grief, even with professional grief counseling and an intensive support system, the wound in one's psyche can remain fresh and bleeding through the years despite intervention. One thing however that can happen is although time does not really heal the grief, the intensity of grieving can ease. Life can take on some degree of significance, like seeds thrown in a wayside, some flourish and bear fruit, others remain stagnant and shriveled, but most will recover and carry on.

In my experience, recollection of what really happened is an important part of the grieving process. This was the most difficult time for us, facing the reality that our only child was physically gone forever. Relating the events from our point of view gives us a chance to share our words and our interpretation of what transpired. We are not saying our judgment is the only truth but we leave it to the reader to make up their own minds and perhaps through our experience they will be extra vigilant when other people are caring for their children. What happened to Mary Jo was almost twenty years ago. Changes in medical care have come a long way. The stigma on special children has eased and now some children with Down syndrome have been well accepted into society and enjoy living a full life. What you are about to read is not to discredit the medical profession. No one is perfect and perhaps it would have been different if Mary Jo was diagnosed properly right from the start

On April 4, 1996 Mary Jo was buried. Mary Jo's funeral was surreal. I could not accept the fact that this beautiful loving, smiling girl who was forever kissing and hugging us first thing in the morning and before sleeping was now a lifeless body inside the small white coffin. She looked like a sleeping angel in a long white dress with lace trimmings. How peaceful she looked. I placed her baptismal candle inside her coffin together with her favourite stuffed toy we called "Sydney." Her hands and whole body remained soft. When her coffin was opened inside the church, there was not a single dry eye among the crowd. The priest, Father Greg must have done a good homily but I could not recall anything except the feeling of helplessness. Joe was steadfast as ever, always protective of me despite the tremendous grief and pain he was carrying.

It was Holy Wednesday when she died and Frank her godfather suggested she should be buried the next day, otherwise with the holidays from Holy Friday up to Easter Monday; Mary Jo's body will just be left cold in the funeral parlour. I wasn't even thinking anymore, I merely complied with what was happening. My mind and body seemed paralysed, unable to feel and think. My friends had to tell me to change clothes and to feed myself. Normal chores seemed beyond me. Fortunately we were blessed with friends Willy and Susan, Elnora, Roger, Frank, Vivian, Noel, Millie, Ross, Rudy and Ophie who handled everything that had to do with the funeral as I was like a zombie. My sister in law, Raquel flew in from America but she didn't make it to the funeral due to the duration of the flight from Los Angeles to

Hell On Earth

Sydney. Our families in the Philippines could only offer long distance support and prayers.

After the funeral, Joe went back to work and I decided to learn more about computing so I could go back to work as well. The emotional challenge was so great that my mentors in school noticed my absent mindedness. I broke down when I told them about Mary Jo's death. Obviously, I hadn't resolved my grief and had been in too much of a hurry to get back into the normal stream of living. My reaction was typical of grievers, the desire to shake off the pain by being busy and preoccupied with day-to-day activities, otherwise the pain can be so confronting.

Finally I was able to openly discuss with a very compassionate chaplain my suspicions that the doctors and the hospital might be liable with the kind of treatment given to Mary Jo, as I was convinced their treatment contributed to her death. I felt so helpless in fighting a formidable battle with the medical team. I have always held medical people in good esteem. Since I was a child, my parents had taught us how helpful doctors and nurses were in helping us to maintain good health. I also have many medical people as friends. I had worked in a pharmaceutical and nutritional company for 18 years going to hospitals, pharmacies, and my interaction with medical people was generally pleasant. I had got on so well with them that I had risen from a hospital sales representative to an Associate Sales Trainer before I left the company. One of my life's highest achievements was winning an award as the Philippines Most Outstanding District Manager in 1991.

Slowly the reverend guided me to remember what had happened. My mind started to remember with amazing clarity the events, procedures, meetings and my feelings in the two weeks prior her death. I had been conscientious in keeping an up-to-date health record for Mary Jo and in the hospital I also kept a diary and it revealed many things that I might have forgotten.

This is the time line of Mary Jo's last two weeks, from

runny nose to death.

Sunday, 17 March 1996

Mary Jo had a runny nose. The specialist had her tonsils and adenoids removed on 22 February 1996 so we made sure she got proper medical attention because of her tonsillectomy. The general practitioner, in his medical opinion advised us nothing was wrong after he checked her lungs and temperature. The doctor advised that due to teething minor flu symptoms can occur.

Monday, 18 March 1996

Part of Mary Jo's intervention plan was to develop her social skills so she was enrolled at a childcare centre to interact with other kids. She seemed better so I brought her to the centre.

Monday, 19 March 1996

Mary Jo had a slight rise in temperature (37.5) and as advised earlier by the general practitioner we gave her an antipyretic and her fever subsided.

Wednesday, 20 March 1996

Mary Jo was not her usual smiling, happy self so we decided to take her to the children's hospital. The attending registrar checked on Mary Jo's temperature and lungs and again said nothing was wrong with her. We requested for Mary Jo to be admitted but again the doctor did not see the need.

Thursday, 21 March 1996

Mary Jo had difficulty in sleeping and instinctively as a mother, I felt something was wrong. Since we could not get Mary Jo to be admitted in the hospital we went back to our general practitioner, who again could not find anything wrong and insisted Mary Jo might just have a viral infection.

Friday, 22 March 1996

Mary slept most of the day and although she did not seem to be in distress, something was worrying me, so I told Joe we have to insist on Mary Jo being admitted. At the casualty ward, the nurse checked her oxygen level and the reading registered low oxygenation. To ease our concern, she said, sometimes the machine didn't work properly. We noticed however, that more medical staff was around Mary Jo. The attending registrar advised she might have pneumonia, which really surprised us as we had been visiting the general practitioner. The staff took an x-ray of Mary Jo's lungs, which confirmed she did indeed have pneumonia. Mary Jo was very agitated and cried loudly as the staff inserted needles into her small wrists. It was apparent she was fighting hard, trying to resist. To hear Mary Jo cry so loud gripped my heart with so much concern as by nature she was never a crying baby. It was around 1:00 am when the attending physician told us Mary Jo will be transported to Intensive Care as she was very sick and needed to be sedated. They told us to leave and come back in the morning. Hesitantly, for the first time in our life, we left Mary Jo in the care of the medical staff as they did not want us to stay overnight in the intensive care.

Saturday, 23 March 1996

We were unprepared to see Mary Jo with so many wires attached to her small body. The doctor confirmed she had a serious chest infection and she had to be intubated to keep her alive. We were shocked to see her condition, with numerous wires connected to monitors. My mind was full of questions; what had they done to Mary Jo the night before? Did they administer morphine because she was crying and fighting before we left? Had they administered a medication that had left her so helpless and dependent on the life support? My mind was numbed; we could not accept the pitiful sight Mary Jo presented. The pediatric cardiologist however gave a bit of hope later in the day when he confirmed there was nothing wrong with Mary Jo's heart.

Sunday, 24 March 1996

Mary Jo's situation deteriorated. She underwent an emergency procedure which I learned later was nitric oxide to help her lung function which they had to use as a last resort to save Mary Jo. Things were deteriorating, and we were now fearful of what the doctors were doing to our daughter.

Monday, 25 March 1996

A peritoneal dialysis was performed and Mary Jo's little body had started to bloat.

Wednesday, 27 March 1996

We were called to attend a conference with the Consultant, the Attending Nurse and a Social Worker. Our friend, Elnora, Mary Jo's godmother and also a Registered Nurse was with us. Before the conference, I learned that the consultant had advised he was afraid Mary Jo had brain damage. The consultant started the conference straight to the point with the chilling assessment that Mary Jo was very sick and had very little chance of survival. He said that, "Mary Jo is so unwell, she had suffered brain damage, her lungs and kidneys were not working and she was not breathing on her own. He further added, any normal two year old with her condition had only 5% chance of survival, but Mary Jo had Down's syndrome and would have even less chance. If her condition improved, she would probably be blind, unable to walk and would never be the way she was before..." He further added, "You have to think of the quality of life in the long run, yes you are capable of loving her now but she will not be able to return that love, she will not be able to interact."

I remembered the medical practitioner who diagnosed Mary Jo at birth and who had told us the worst things about having a child with Down's syndrome. I wanted to cry and, I wanted to know if they had tried experimental treatments and procedures on my child, which was why she had gone down so fast?

The social worker was so cold and simply said, "You have to make a decision in favour of the child."

Unable to contain my anger, I replied, "What kind of decision do you mean; a kind of decision that will put our daughter under the ground? We know our daughter wants to be in the arms of her loving parents, that's why she was crying so loudly before she was admitted."

Joe added, "Even if my daughter doesn't walk or talk, we will take her home. Even just to see her breathing and for us to smell her presence, we will be happy to take care of her. Please do not cut off the life support for as long as she can still breathe. Remember you revive 80 year old patients; Mary Jo is only two years old."

The social worker was relentless in what she wanted to achieve when she said, "So many parents do that, then after two or three years they dump their kids in institutions. We have experienced that already. You have to see the future of your daughter." I could hardly believe what was being said, had these people already decided to let Mary Jo die?

Joe replied, "If I could not take care of my daughter, my sister would, my friend Elnora will take care of Mary Jo, other family members will do the same. We just do not give up. I provided for my father until he died at the age of eighty four how much more for my very own daughter?"

It was then very apparent they wanted our consent to turn off the life support system. Boldly I told the medical staff, "We don't belong to a culture that believes in euthanasia. We do not have this kind of social welfare in our country, the Philippines, but we care in our hearts, in our emotions. Families look after each other. Please don't take off our daughter from the respirator even if she is just taking 10% oxygen, let us wait until her system can't take anything anymore."

The consultant seemed unmoved. He simply said, "Our duty is primarily for the patients." I wanted to scream when I heard this; luckily, I had the decency to stay quiet.

I thought Joe would hit the Social Worker when she said, "Why don't you go home and make another baby?"

The male nurse, who seemed the only sympathetic

person in the room, summed up the meeting by saying, "Let Mary Jo decide for herself."

We had not slept for days, and since we saw Mary Jo's condition, Joe and I decided not to leave her totally in the care of the medical staff. We watched their every move day and night. Later, we saw Mary Jo move her hand and blink her eyes. It was a temporary relief as we learned later they had administered a morphine reversal drug. On the afternoon of the same day, a neurologist was called. I was surprised when he announced after a neurological assessment, "If this baby had no pneumonia she could get up and go." Now I was really angry, as early in the morning we were told Mary Jo had brain damage even before a neurological assessment had been done.

Thursday, 28 March 1996.

The neurologist gave us a bit of hope when he said, "The brain scan result is okay, no bleeding, no swelling, no lumps, and she has no epilepsy and will hopefully recover.

Friday, 29 March 1996

The staff opened a line in Mary Jo's neck and did a hemodialysis. We were told that the peritoneal dialysis was not working. It was also Joe's birthday. Mary Jo was stable.

Sunday, 31 March 1996

The consultant was off duty. A young medical officer called us for a meeting and said, "You might have a dead baby tonight. Pneumonia is now the least of your concerns, Mary Jo's organs are shutting down from the side effects of the treatment. Another senior doctor took over the next shift and repeated, "You know your daughter is dying. My mind was reeling with disbelief, anger had seeped into my whole being, what have they done?

Monday, 1 April 1996

Another scan was done on Mary Jo. She had bouts of low oxygenation. It was now almost a week since Joe and I had started to watch Mary Jo day and night, as we no longer trusted the medical staff. We were so afraid we might just find Mary Jo dead.

Tuesday, 2 April 1996

Mary Jo again had bouts of low blood pressure and very irregular breathing. With so much grief in my heart, I whispered to Mary Jo, "We love you so much and we will do everything to keep you alive. However, we know only Jesus and you can decide now. We don't want you to suffer but we want you to always remember how much we love you." I saw a single big tear fall on Mary Jo's left eye. I was shaking with grief. Joe later told me, that even inside the elevator; he would kneel down on his knees and beg God to spare the life of our only child.

Wednesday, 3 April

Early in the morning, a tube was inserted into Mary

Jo's lungs to drain the fluid. She died at 10:25 in the morning.

To this day, I can still clearly see Joe, crying helplessly as he embraced our lifeless daughter. I was so numbed, as if I was experiencing a nightmare in front of my eyes. If there was hell, that day must be the day when all hell broke loose and claimed whatever sense of faith and confidence we had with the medical system.

Years have passed since that hellish day. Eventually, it was our Catholic faith that provided comfort and helped give us the determination not to live as victims of grief, or as victims of the medical and judicial system.

Almost Magical Synchronicity in Abundance

The future depends on what we do in the present
Mahatma Gandhi
~*~

A loss and grief experience can make the griever feel as though there is only a thin line between crazy and normal. Fantasy and reality seem fused into one at certain times. In my early student days I marveled at the theories based on scientific proofs, clinical findings and laboratory tests results. The advent of more sophisticated technology is no doubt interesting but I have also seen the futility of science in proving that which cannot be seen, or reproduced, or altered in the laboratory. Dreams and coincidences are among life's daily occurrences but fully understanding the essence of dreams and synchronized happenings in our physical word is still a challenge these days. Simple everyday occurrences highlight this reality. For instance, we do not see air or energy, yet the presence or absence of them can make a lot of difference to our existence.

No matter what differences people have in culture or beliefs, the majority still look up to a Divine Creator to help us out of misery. Most share the common belief that there is a heaven for good men and women. Many also believe that we are interconnected to each other, even between the living and those in the spirit world. A mother of an unborn child can feel the presence of this tiny creature, the life growing inside her belly. A child, no matter how young, can immediately identify the carer who nurtures them. Powerful emotions of love, hate, helplessness, anger or hope cannot be seen by the naked eye but human beings do understand how these feelings can occupy their thoughts and even drive them into actions

Almost Magical Synchronicity in Abundance

~*~

favorable or not for themselves and those around them. These days spirituality is no longer confined to the limiting boundaries of religions, culture or anything that separates human beings; but concepts of a loving, caring, nurturing heart, hopes for a better future, belief in an indomitable human spirit links us all. More than any other period in my life, I have witnessed and felt this synchronicity of events, the occurrence of dreams and spiritual guidance shared by friends, family and acquaintances, personal and professional, who had dealings with us and Mary Jo during her brief time on earth.

Looking back, I can now recall with amazing clarity the events surrounding the dreams, coincidences and synchronicity that related to Mary Jo, our only child who was so untimely taken from us.

In my body and my soul, I was tired with grief. The intensity of so much grief can be overwhelming. Words cannot fully express the feelings of sadness, helplessness, hopelessness and the inability to feel even a flutter of hope for better tomorrows. Out of despair, unexpectedly rainbows can appear, mostly in dreams and coincidences. Science cannot fully explain how the conscious, unconscious and the alignment of body, mind, soul and spirit works in unison with collective consciousness and the universal mind. The quest for knowledge and explanation can be futile for what is physically invisible, but its presence in our thoughts, psyche and emotions cannot be ignored. The word synchronicity was something I had not understood fully before. I only had a vague idea that when things are synchronized, like synchronized swimming, synchronized timing, and synchronized dancing, there is beauty, harmony and order. The graceful movements of swimmers and dancers always had me mesmerized. When I was eight years old, I was a young violinist and I played in my first orchestra, and I was amazed at how our violin teacher could pick up even one unsynchronized note. Even though I did not develop my skills in dancing and in playing the violin, the need for synchronicity had been instilled in my long-term memory. More than 50

Almost Magical Synchronicity in Abundance

years after I played the violin, synchronicity of events fell into place with more clarity. This time I realized how interconnected, events, people and the multidimensional universe, the divine and the spirit world could be. Mary Jo's death had opened a floodgate of awakenings for my body, heart, mind and soul. For eighteen years, I hid from knowing it, by burying myself in hard work within a corporate life, yet things kept occurring until I was ready to face it.

The first dream I had shortly after Mary Jo's funeral was seeing her sitting at the edge of my bed and she was looking at me with tears in her eyes. I woke up with intense sadness, no longer for myself, but as a mother, I wanted to protect Mary Jo from the pain of being separated from me physically. The dream of her was recurring night after night. I wished to be where she was, in spirit with her instead of being chained to the limitations of my physical body. There were times, even on public transport; I would burst into tears as I was missing our daughter terribly. One night, I dreamt of her again, this time she held out her two chubby hands and instinctively I saw myself reaching out to her. I felt a strong pull towards her, as if she was pulling me closer and closer. I saw myself getting out of bed and I caught a glimpse of my husband Joe sleeping beside me. I told her not to take me yet as poor Papa will be left all alone. Instantly, I felt disengaged from her strong pull, waking up to intense chest pain and I realized I could have died of a heart attack.

No doubt, I panicked with the realization that my death wish could be a reality. I can still recall the feeling of intense chest pain and a very tight squeeze in my upper body. That must be the feeling of a helpless person under the weight of big elephant. I was cold and felt lightheaded. I was feeling like a rag doll without much command of my body. While the dream made me feel uncomfortable, it reinforced my belief that spirits are alive and well, knowing how we feel in the physical world. I am convinced that Mary Jo is always around me and is helping me cope with my chronic sorrow and she wanted to help me then by

Almost Magical Synchronicity in Abundance

literally pulling my soul to where she was, in the spiritual realm.

In my intense sorrow, I had become oblivious to Joe's plight if he became a widower only a few weeks after losing an only child. The pain that night sent shivers down my spine, knowing that even if I would be in spirit, I did not want to see him in extreme pain again.

I had started to look forward to my bedtime. In my dreams, I can feel and see my daughter. In one beautiful dream, I saw my face cupped between Mary Jo's familiar chubby and soft hands, I saw her beautiful face, and the feeling I had was like she was the comforter and I the little child that needed assurance. Mary Jo clearly delivered the message, "You are permanently and forever my mother." I think I had that dream because although I was mentally comforted with the visualization that an Angel Mother with the supervision of the Blessed Virgin Mary was taking care of her, deep inside, I was still angry and jealous that my mother role was taken away so soon. Then Joe started dreaming of Mary Jo too. He said in one episode, he saw a tall, well-built but faceless figure, communicating through his mind. He also saw Mary Jo as if protected by a dome of white light. Then in Joe's mind, he recalled asking the figure, "Why is our daughter still here when we have already buried her?"

The figure replied; "She does not want to go up yet as she wanted to take good care of Papa and Mama."

I felt so much anguish upon hearing this from Joe. While I greatly appreciated our daughter's depth of compassion and love for us, I was aware our grief was selfishly delaying her from her beautiful, painless, happiness filled life in heaven. One day, I caught Joe in a pensive mood. I asked him to tell me what was bothering him. He told me, that in a dream, Mary Jo had said, "Papa, the doctors didn't know what they were doing."

The drama of life and death is no doubt the most gut wrenching experience any mortal can have and to get a message from the grave to confirm my suspicions was like sharp arrows hitting my already shattered heart. I could only console Joe with the reality that medical practitioners are also human beings, just like we are, subject to imperfections but at the end of day only God has the power to take lives away. My faith had plummeted to its lowest level after Mary Jo's death but strangely, I can feel it starting to build up again and in essence is to this day, my wellspring of hope and determination to find meaning in losing a much-wanted only child.

Joe's emotional vulnerability was wearing thin. Our neighbor told me, with much concern, that Joe was crying when he visited them and that Joe told them he could not afford to look vulnerable and emotionally weak, as he knew I needed him for support. How sad it is, that most men feel they have to put up a strong front when they are also crumbling. Our neighbor's well-meaning revelation made me ponder on how blind I was to Joe's inner pain of losing not only his daughter but his lifetime role as a father. He had been trying to be a super hero for me. Joe is a martial arts expert, a black belt in aikido, a real man's man but I was oblivious to the tender hearted, emotionally broken man, he was after losing Mary Jo. I looked back on how my own father, grandfather and other male family members handle grief. I had not seen them cry when I was a child. I had seen my younger brothers cry as children but looking back Joe was the first male I have ever seen cry unashamedly as he cuddled our lifeless child. It was also the first time I realized how powerless a grieving father can be when confronted with the futility of death. It was Joe who first broke down with a big cry when the nurse confirmed Mary Jo's death. I can clearly recall the unspeakable feeling I had to see Joe wailing as he clutched Mary Jo's lifeless body. I was frozen then, unable to speak, I could not even move. All I heard were Joe's cries as he vented his anger at God. The scene was so unreal; here was my husband who earlier had been so devoted and grateful because he was finally a family man. Like the proverbial thief in the night, his cherished role as a father had been taken from him. I have many poignant memories of Joe with Mary Jo. Once when he was sick with severe bronchitis, he was groggy from medication, and half asleep when he was awakended with Mary Jo's tight hug. She held his face tight and kissed him on the lips as if absorbing everything from him. Joe also gave up smoking for Mary Jo. He had been a heavy smoker for over 25 years, yet when I became pregnant he made it a point to only smoke either on the small balcony or outside of the apartment. He had tried everything to stop smoking, patches, meditation and abstinence but none had held. He told me that what stopped him finally was when he noticed a tear in Mary Jo's t-shirt, and he felt so bad that he spent money on cigarettes instead of new outfits for his daughter. In the short time that Mary Jo lived, she idolized her father. She had amused us with her expertise in throwing karate kicks and punches, she even had a karate outfit and in many ways it was obvious she was a good mimic of Joe's martial arts prowess. There were happy times when Mary Jo and her Papa danced to the tune of

"True Love." In the 1980's that song had mesmerized me. The lyrics told of having a guardian angel that had nothing to do but to watch and make sure that we had true love. I could not understand why the vision of a guardian angel watching a couple to make sure true love binds them had kept me company for many years. The emotional tension caused by grieving and the absence of a smiling happy child was unbearable. We had many happy dreams for the future that revolved around Mary Jo but all those dreams ended on the day she died. Joe was immobilized too; the reality of losing our only child continues to affect us in different ways, even to this day.

One evening, sadness gripped me again. I must have fallen asleep crying and there I saw a very beautiful but authoritative little Mary Jo, saying in exasperation, "but Mama, I don't have blood anymore." I woke up amused with that dream and was pleasantly surprised with my reflections. Perhaps, Mary Jo must have sensed how much I wanted her to come back, yet in my heart, I knew it was irrational for me to keep on wishing that she could. Then, the next night, Mary Jo appeared again, pointing at the stars she said, "I am now a form of energy just like them." It was a very comforting dream, even now, I still look up the stars and comfort myself with the idea that Mary Jo is shining more brightly than ever. One day I saw some schoolchildren on their way home. How I envied the mothers who will welcome home their children, give them big hugs then talk about what had happened in school. It reminded me of my grade school days at a Catholic school. As I had not had the chance to dress up my own child and send her to school; I imagined Mary Jo to be around six years old and being schooled by angels in heaven. Shortly after, I dreamt about her in a school uniform and being taught her lessons. It was not like our normal way of teaching children. It was as if Mary Jo was being transported to an actual happening. The scene was so real in my dream; Mary Jo was watching intently as a woman in white explained what was unfolding before her. What a way to learn, I can imagine that this is the way children are schooled in heaven, they get to witness the real event, not a recreation, but the real thing. I felt I was being educated too, that in heaven, past, present and future can all happen at once. Another incident was on a cold winter day, as I passed a shop I saw on the display window a beautiful matching hat and cape for a little girl. I knew that if Mary Jo were alive I would surely dress her in that outfit. I went home; feeling drained, and again fell asleep. I dreamt of Mary Jo, wearing a little red riding hood cape with matching hood her face framed beautifully with pink flowerets. I woke up convinced there is indeed an alignment of the conscious and subconscious mind.

Synchronicity and coincidences started to happen with more frequency. One morning I slept late and waking up to an empty crib beside me started crying uncontrollably. I allowed myself to have a good cry as Joe had gone to work and I was all alone in the house. The phone rang, suddenly, so I tried to compose myself so the caller would not know I was in tears. It

Almost Magical Synchronicity in Abundance

was Christy, one of staff from the hospital where Mary Jo died. She said she woke up and saw Mary Jo climb up in her bed with her and in her mind, she was told to call me because I was crying. I did not believe that Christy would make up the story; it was too coincidental, because I was indeed crying my heart out. Christy had been on duty since day one of Mary Jo's admission in the paediatric intensive care unit. She would volunteer to watch Mary Jo, with Joe, during her lunch break, as she knew I would want to go to the nearby church for a few minutes so I could pray for Mary Jo's life to be spared. During the 15 to 20 minutes I had at the church, I begged God to take my life instead of Mary Jo's. I knew I might not be able to cope with Mary Jo's death but my prayers were not answered the way I wanted. I had appreciated Christy's presence during those times. Sot that Christy could hang up I promised her that I wouldn't cry for the rest of the day. Later, Christy revealed to me that after Mary Jo was buried, when she was on early morning shifts, there were many times she saw Mary Jo visiting her hospital bed but she was not afraid, as she had seen other departed children make a visit after their death. One remarkable woman, we simply call "Mommy" who is a grandmother to an autistic child, told me she had a very vivid dream of Mary Jo. Eagerly she told me that one evening after she prayed her nightly rosary, she must have fallen into a trance, a dream state while still kneeling in in front of her homemade altar. She said she saw Mary Jo as a sixteen year old, tall, slim, a long haired young lady dressed in an almost cloud like white outfit smiling at her and saying, "Tell Mama this is how I look now." Tears fell from my eyes and I sobbed uncontrollably because the day before I had wanted to have a vision of Mary Jo as a young woman. How in the world did this kind woman have the vision, which was the very answer to what I wanted to see? Mommy described with much clarity how beautiful Mary Jo had grown and how clear was her request to let me know her message. That dream of Mommy started more revelations from close friends

Almost Magical Synchronicity in Abundance

~*~

and family who had known her.

Back home my own mother Salvacion was also getting messages from Mary Jo. As a grieving grandmother, her only source of strength was to go to church and seek solace in prayers. One day while talking to me on the phone, she said she must have fallen asleep while praying the day before because she clearly remembered Mary Jo between her knees, smiling and happily touching her face. She wanted to touch her back but seemed frozen and could not move. In another incident, my mother recalled that they had a new laundry woman, who has the same Christian name "Lourdes" as mine. During that time, my mother was living with my brother Gerry who had two sons, John Gerald and Carlos. My mother said that Lourdes was upset one day and she asked why my mother and the rest of the family were unmindful of a beautiful girl whom she sees tugging at my mother's dress every morning as my mother has her coffee. The laundry woman said she had seen the child a number of times but no one seems to pay attention to her, and she felt bad that the child was being ignored. My mother asked her for more details, and convinced that Mary Jo was appearing to Lourdes, my mother got the photo album and asked Lourdes if the child in the pink and white dress was the child she saw. Lourdes confirmed indeed it was the same kind of outfit the child was wearing. My Mom hugged her and delivered the unbelievable news that the child she was seeing was in fact her granddaughter, Mary Jo, dead and buried in Sydney, Australia. Years later, when my mother was in Leyte, an island in the Philippines, she had another clear dream of Mary Jo. In her dream, she saw Mary Jo had sewn together some eggs like a giant wreath and was dragging the egg wreath to her. When my Mom told me of that dream I immediately thought it was Mary Jo's funny way of telling all the family members to always stay connected to each other. Whether that was the message of the dream or not, I had formed the habit of immediately paying attention to the idea or impact of what was being told to me. My mom

Almost Magical Synchronicity in Abundance

always loved to cook and our childhood days had made our kitchen the busiest place in the house. My Mom was so grateful for a particular cake recipe she said Mary Jo had given her. In the dream, she was shown the different ingredients but no specified quantities or units of measurement. She tried the mixture and it turned out be the tastiest cake she had ever baked. One of Mary Jo's godmother, Elnora, is my best friend. She was almost like Mary Jo's second mother. She is to this day, a strong pillar of support and still cries when we remember Mary Jo. She had a dream of Mary Jo supporting her in a real estate venture as she said she was unsure and had asked for Mary Jo's guidance. The most notable intervention of Mary Jo was in the life of another very close friend Ophie who had been divorced and was living with us temporarily. Joe and I jokingly told Ophie she should get married again. How strongly she denied even the prospect of dating as she said she had more than enough bad experiences. One day while we were at Mary Jo's grave, we asked her to help Auntie Ophie

A Kiss From An Angel

gets a good man to marry. One day Ophie and I went to a sale of clothes in a fashion warehouse. I saw this beautiful white cocktail dress. For unknown reasons I was forceful with my opinion that Ophie should buy the dress as it was heavily discounted. Ophie didn't want to buy it, as she did not see the need for it so I offered to buy it for her. Good friend that she is and to keep the peace with me, she bought the item still mumbling it will just go into her pile of unused clothes. We forgot all about it then one day, we noticed an unusual sprightliness in Ophie's character. She looked happier and Joe and I suspected she might be secretly dating. Not long after, Ophie moved out of our place admitting she was moving in with a new guy. When she married him, the long abandoned white cocktail dress we bought in a warehouse sale became her wedding gown. Mary Jo's growing influence as an intercessor and helper was getting wider among our circle of friends and family. One evening, another very close friend Wayne, told me that he kept Mary Jo's picture by his bedside. He reported that one time he had asked Mary Jo to help him with some challenges and was so grateful that Mary Jo appeared in his dream. He said he saw Mary Jo, still as a toddler but with a very authoritative persona. He saw himself spell bound and obedient when Mary Jo showed him strong cement wall and commanded, "Go through that wall." A few days after that dream, he found a way out of his problem. When Mary Jo was alive, Wayne was like a dotting grandpa. Every last Saturday of November as a thanksgiving for her brief and meaningful life, we still celebrate her birthday. It is a time for us to reconnect with wonderful people who knew Mary Jo and are still very much a part of our lives. Wayne is a gifted musician and often he sings Mary Jo's favourite song True Love and plays the guitar as accompaniment.

Mary Jo has another godfather, Frank. When Mary Jo was dying in the hospital, Frank was a frequent visitor offering us much support and a great listener when we expressed our frustrations. Frank had the unpleasant task of arranging Mary Jo's funeral. He was like a big brother, keeping a careful eye on me in the following days. Unexpectedly Frank had a serious illness and sadly, he informed Joe and me he might not survive. We prayed for Frank's health to improve. Frank told us two days before his doctor's appointment, he dreamt of Mary Jo appearing with a beautiful woman. In his dream, he saw Mary Jo request that the woman put her hand on his forehead so he will be cured. When he went to see his doctor, the doctor almost fell off his chair to see the symptoms of his serious illness gone. Later, we attributed the beautiful woman with Mary Jo to be the Blessed Mother. Since then Frank has felt Mary Jo's presence more often. At that time, we did not own a home and we were house hunting. Finally, we settled on the small property where we are living now. What was significant was we were able to close the property deal in November, which was Mary Jo's birth month. Frank had told us he could not understand why he dreamt of Mary Jo saying, "Tell Papa and Mama, I have searched all over Sydney for that house." Amazed, we told Frank that we actually asked Mary Jo to look for a house for us, not far from where she was buried so we can visit her. By coincidence, it was Frank's friend, mother to a real estate agent who had recommended the house to us and facilitated a very good deal. Another dream that Frank had was the night Mary Jo told him to get up and go with her. He said "how can I go with you, I don't have wings." Mary Jo grabbed him by the hand and led him to a beautiful country house with a big garden, full of evergreen and lush leafed plants. Frank said, they went up a wooden spiral staircase and Mary Jo showed him a beautiful room furnished with mostly white furnishings, the curtains were shimmering white, transparent and of the finest fabric. The bed was dressed in the most beautiful bed covers he had ever seen and he said in his mind he was looking for toys but could not find any. Then he woke up. He visited us, as he could not understand why he had that dream of Mary Jo showing him the most beautiful country home and bedroom he had ever seen.

Earlier I had told Frank I was depressed to think how much we had wanted to provide Mary Jo with a good future but her death robbed us of this dream. Frank, more composed and the big brother that he was to us, said, "Lulu, I have been to the houses of kings and queens and royalty in the Middle East, I have travelled extensively around the world and I have been to the best places in America and Europe but nothing compares to the beauty and comfort of the place where your daughter lives now. When I learned about his dream I had goose bumps, how amazing to realize that Frank was noticing the same dream I had, of a country home were we could have lived with Mary Jo. I hadn't even described such a wish to Joe and the immense longing to see Mary Jo enjoy a holiday home in the country, but there was Frank a profound witness that our minds can be so interconnected in a psychic sphere. From 1996 to now, 2014, more dreams and synchronicities had been noted; even the writing of this book seemed to have been pre-programmed. For more than eighteen

Almost Magical Synchronicity in Abundance

years, I had kept my memorabilia of Mary Jo hidden away, almost unreachable, and then one day my mentor, Pam, asked me to look for clear photo of Mary Jo. After almost a day of searching through stored boxes, I found a minefield of documents, doctor's reports, old diaries and photos, baby things. Memories flooded in, as if everything that happened since her birth in 1993 to now were all encapsulated for easy recall. Repressing memories of Mary Jo was a way of protecting me from grief; it had been my way of coping. In 2012, I took up serious studies and came across, Carl Jung a Swiss psychiatrist who said, *"An individual is precisely that which can never be merged with the collective and is never identical with it."* His books and his experiences as a Psychologist showed me that there is a great collective unconscious, as well as a collective conscious, and his work stands up to scientific scrutiny. What a big relief to realize that dreams, coincidences, synchronicities are real and indeed have a place in the scientific world. The greatest thing I learnt is that when we go on a journey where our conscious, subconscious mind, body, soul and spirit are aligned, we can feel life's meaning in a way we never have before. Through this journey, I now know that the death of our only child enhances my commitment to live, and that even now we are still connected.

Application of Theories on Grieving

The journey of a thousand miles must begin with a single step. **Lao Tzu**

~*~

This year again shows evidence of synchronicity. Mary Jo would be turning 21 years old on November 23, 2014; I will receive my Post Graduate in Counseling Degree on 21, November 2014 just two days before her birthday. It was because of my chronic grief that I studied counseling, perhaps my graduation date and the closeness of her 21st birthday is telling me once more, she is looking after us.

One of the important lessons I learnt was from Kubler-Ross, and her 'Five stages of Grief' (1969).

Anger, Denial, Bargaining, Depression and Acceptance. This new level of understanding helped me analyze myself as I experienced grief again when I saw my own mother dying and doctors were telling us she would lose her life. My experience with Mary Jo gave me courage to logically deal with the medical team. I asked to stay inside the intensive care room of my mother and for two weeks, I never left the premises. My two other brothers, Peter and Michael took turns to partner with me during the evenings. Many times, we were told that the laboratory tests were showing the futility of letting my mother continue on the life support system. My initial reaction to the news was one of shock, followed by anger. Fierce anger can surface when we are confronted with an upcoming death. Anger can be so irrational and displaced. Some people vent their anger on anyone and on anything. Blaming also falls on medical personnel, support workers and anyone who might be involved. I was frustrated, anxious and irritated that we had no control on what was happening. It was embarrassing

Application of Theories on Grieving

as well to admit that I was ill equipped to admit the reality of death, I was in denial that it could occur. The third stage according to Kubler-Ross was bargaining. I was reaching out to as many family and friends as I could to help me pray to God with greater intensity, to bargain that we will be spared another death in the family. In the fourth stage, depression can sit in. I was feeling so overwhelmed with grief to see my mother hovering between life and death. Perhaps the lack of sleep, loss of appetite and the grim scenario of death happening anytime had taken its toll on me again. Towards the end of the second week, we were fully convinced we had done everything for our mother; we called the priest to do the last rites for the dying. In a strange and happy twist of fate, came the last stage of acceptance that anything can happen. My mother survived and is still very much around at the age of 84.

Grief is not a linear movement. When I was at the hospital, I saw children being treated and these triggered memories of Mary Jo being so helpless. I was also confronted with the miscarriage, eight months after Mary Jo's death. The mind can be merciless in remembering previous occasions and triggering the grief again. I hated to see smiling babies being cradled by their mothers. It reminded me how I felt before, abandoned by God as he ignored my prayers for Mary Jo's life and for a successful pregnancy

I dedicated myself to studying the concepts of grief while I was in school. Acceptance is the last stage of the grief process, and acceptance about Mary Jo's death started when I was learning more in postgraduate studies. Kubler-Ross (1975) stated that *death provides a greater meaning for human existence.* The concept was so paradoxical but I learned to understand that because we realize there is so much in life we cannot control, then it was a good thing to appreciate and be grateful for the life we have and love ones who are living. It was a long time for me to finally accept that Mary Jo and the baby we named Theresa Rose, whom we lost in miscarriage are still very much around, not in physical state but in a spiritual state.

Complicated grief as cited by Parkes and Weiss (1983) *is unresolved, abnormal grief that happens when recovery fails to take place.* It is good to understand that as humans, we can all have different experiences of grief, symptoms can strike with different intensity and at times we least expect. The loss of a child is definitely one of the most painful tragedies any parent can experience. This kind of grief can become so entrenched in ourselves that its freshness re-occurs with multiple triggers throughout our lives. Kastebaum, (1996) cited that bereavement overload can happen when people have multiple losses. To pretend that everything is under control can be devastating to grievers. It is suggested that when people are affected with intense grief they may show symptoms like low blood pressure, frequent headaches, and uncontrolled sadness and crying episodes and it is highly recommended for these people to seek professional help. Some people can be driven to suicidal tendencies, to take on maladaptive habits and never recover. Others become serious drug addicts, alcoholics and others simply bury themselves with work and other adrenalin driven pursuits. Relationship with themselves and love ones can be damaged. Incidents of road rage and violence can also occur if grief continues to be repressed,

Intense grieving however is not a hopeless case. One clinician Carr (2007) advised *that when people have a deep and lasting attachment, happiness is not farfetched*. We see friendships and the relationship of couples reach a higher level of intimacy because grief has brought them together. As social beings, grief and happy moments can create a strong bond. To date, I have maintained close friendships with people who were there for us when Mary Jo was sick and during the bleak moments of her death. Death, grief and loss are not easy to overcome but they can be a positive force in not taking our lives and our love ones for granted.

Children born with disabilities can also cause

Application of Theories on Grieving

immense grief for unsuspecting parents. Mothers who have aborted their babies due to chromosomal abnormalities and other reasons grieve, some openly and others in secret due to shame and guilt. Parents with disabled children are sometimes unprepared to care for a child with a disability. Although the child is alive, some parents feel that they are deprived of their dreams, hopes, expectations and the assumption of having healthy, happy grandchildren. There is some similarity of acceptance for the death of a well love child, one with a disability and an unseen one because of miscarriage. The child I lost in miscarriage did not reached full developmental stage; our happiness that I was pregnant again was quickly dashed with the miscarriage. The roller coaster ride of emotional upheaval of excitement due to pregnancy, the lows of knowing a child has disability then later to experience miscarriage is not for the faint hearted. I had gone to the lowest level of my emotions, and I still feel the sense of tremendous loss. Anyone confronted with grief needs to seek support. There are other challenges that affects parents like their socio-economic status, availability or lack of support systems, having other children in the home, religious beliefs or none at all, different cultural attitudes towards children with disability and other prognosis, all these factors can greatly affect the grieving process.

What can be done when someone is grieving? First, it is best to understand that grieving is different for every person. I can only cite my own personal experience, which though not an easy one had made me learn to really embrace life now with appreciation and gratitude. I have mentioned in this book that there are symptoms to contend with. Physical symptoms can range from a feeling of heaviness, uncontrolled crying, always feeling tired, and pain all over the body. Emotionally, one can feel sadness so intense that it can trigger thoughts of suicide. Socially people may isolate themselves, there was a time I did not want to meet my high school friends who were living in another state and who just wanted to know

Application of Theories on Grieving

how things were going with me. The sadness and yearning was so bad; I didn't want to share it with anyone. Spiritually, one is also challenged but later you may realize that faith is a way to remain rational and hopeful that not everything has ended. Some grievers can become so depressed and develop post-traumatic stress disorder that this can greatly affect family life and the griever's physical and emotional health.

People who are grieving can be helped by encouraging them to talk about how they feel, try to listen, to understand and not to immediately give advice as they just need to express their feelings, share their memories. It is also important to help grievers in practical ways, like helping with household chores, doing some cooking and gardening for them, encourage them to seek professional help and even to visit doctors if their health is deteriorating. There is no fixed formula for grieving. As I observed, time does not completely take away the grief but over a period of time grievers can adjust and life can take on a new meaning.

I will forever be grateful to Mary Jo for so many things. Foremost is the beautiful vision of what must be heaven. In my dream, I saw her as a young woman and surprisingly I too am young. There is no verbal exchange but like most dreams of her, it seems like mind-to-mind communication. It was a beautiful a dream, I felt so good knowing I was beside my daughter and we were gliding through waterfalls, and the most beautiful garden and woodlands. The waterfall was not cascading with water but almost like mystical white clouds and the flowers were big and mostly of pinkish salmon in shades. I saw her in a long white outfit, very similar to the angelic outfit on the cover of this book. Pam, the person who designed the cover in October 2014 felt immediately that the design on the cover was the most appropriate. It is really hard to fathom out how in 1996, Mommy the old lady also described the same outfit in her dream of Mary Jo, and it is the same description from Uncle Peter last September and Frank, her godfather also

Application of Theories on Grieving

saw Mary Jo in the same long white gown. How five people at different times can have the same description of Mary Jo's outfits at different times and in different places just seem so unbelievable. Coincidentally after my dream of her near the waterfalls, the next day a friend invited me to Tao Chinese worship. The event was more of a multicultural gathering acknowledging the presence of heaven but not interpreted as exclusive to only one religion. One man kept on mentioning the river of life and asked me if I had a concept of it, then I told him my dream of Mary Jo and me gliding through the waterfalls and the riverbeds with so many wild beautiful flowers. I was surprised when he said, "Indeed you have seen the river of life in heaven."

I can write pages and pages of memories now about Mary Jo. As if all of a sudden the floodgates of memory have opened since Pam showed me the cover of the book. Just last night I was reminded of my dream where I saw her and a small girl, hugging and kissing me. Then in my mind, I didn't have any recollection at all that Mary Jo was dead and that I had a miscarriage. In my dream I know they were my daughters and I was hugging them back, the three of us so happily engulfed in a threesome embrace, then after a while, I saw Mary Jo's chubby face, with eyes so alive and sparkling, then in the sweetest but very happy and clear voice she said, "Mama, we can't stay long…J E S U S is waiting for us." Then I woke up, though sad both my daughters were only in my dream, I felt so comforted. Some clinicians attest that dreams are mythical, an offshoot of what our conscious mind wants and the subconscious reflects back. I didn't really care what interpretation my dreams could have had, one thing I felt though was how comforting the thought was, that no less than Jesus was taking care of them until I get to heaven too.

On the 23 November 2012, I was in our classroom and the topic for the day was "Forgiveness", our educator was explaining to us the effects of forgiveness in maintaining good mental health and in

Application of Theories on Grieving

minimizing conflicts in life. Our class was full of ambivalent ideas, some were in disagreement and highly critical of forgiveness. When I was asked what my opinion was, my mind went back to the scene when I was told by the young doctor, that pneumonia was the least of their concern, as from all probability she was suffering from the side effects of treatment. I said in a clear voice, I have forgiven all those responsible for my daughter's death in 1996, and then I briefly explained what had happened. There wasn't a dry eye in our classroom. We started to hug each other including our teacher and everyone gave credit to Mary Jo's story as the essence of forgiveness in action. From that moment, I also felt a lightness I have never felt before, connectivity with the rest of our class and our educator. When I got my grades at the end of the semester, I was happy to get a high distinction in the subject were forgiveness was made clear and relevant to mental health with Mary Jo's story.

I believe Mary Jo must be partly responsible for all

these synchronicity of events that are leading and connecting all of us, a link from God, or from the Universe to remind us mortals that heaven is not just a figment of our imagination but like our spirit it is as real as what we can see here on earth, and that the souls of our departed loved ones never forget their loved ones on earth.

Transforming Grief into Gifts

You must be the change you want to see in the world.
Mahatma Ghandi
~*~

There are three things that most people share regardless of race, colour, belief and social condition of life; the joy brought by the birth of a new life, the unfathomable pain that can result from grief and loss of love ones and the transformations in life at different times due to the outcome of grief and loss. Grief and loss is a reality most people have to face. Personally, I realized the importance of having faith, of believing that there is an awesome, mighty God who created heaven, earth and us. Faith is in believing what is unseen and yet can be felt. Just because Mary

Jo isn't around physically doesn't mean she no longer exist. She may be a form of energy, a star in the sky, an angel who always guides me, yet whatever form, I have learned to accept that she is never far away and would want to see me move on with life. My Catholic faith had always maintained, that we are but mystical beings just being given the opportunity to become human beings and in due time we will come back to our pure spiritual state once we die. The reality that I can say, I am a mother to an angel makes me feel so proud and humble at the same time. As a human mother, I realized I am so powerless when death beckons yet I feel I am so gifted with a strong spirit that knows hope and what it means to trust in God's plan for all His creations.

~*~

1 Corinthians 13:4–8a

Love is patient, love is kind. It does not envy, it does not boast, it is not proud. It is not rude, it is not self-seeking, it is not easily angered, and it keeps no record of wrongs. Love does not delight in evil but rejoices with the truth. It always protects, always trusts, always hopes, and always perseveres. Love never fails.

~*~

Amidst all the pain that grief and loss can bring, love is an empowering emotion that can make us realize how important life is. It is so tempting to forget love and give vent to anger and hatred, to continue to blame anyone or anything that could have a role in the death of a love one.

After a while, we realize that we and the people we blame are all powerless when the time for dying comes. No amount of medical intervention or even the love we have for a love one can extend the limited life everyone has. It is with this realization that I am very grateful for the brief time I had as a mother. Loving doesn't end with death; in fact, death makes the loving even more meaningful. Joe and I had realized that in order for us to survive the cruelty of grief, we needed to love and to care for each other more. No one else can feel the intensity of our love for Mary Jo and the heartfelt devastation in our emotional life because of the void her death had left. This kind of love has intensified because we have learned to understand each other even more. Our love and understanding had made us more compassionate to other people in the grip of grief.

In an article I had written for the South Sydney Herald for their October 7, 2014 issue, titled "Too much love, too little time", I mentioned, "Loving and caring is a universal language that everyone understands and aspires for. The loving care of our carers, be they biologically connected to us or not, nurses human beings from conception to birth, during our most productive years, even when death approaches, these loving and caring people make a lot of difference in our existence."

Mary Jo was diagnosed with Down's syndrome, a condition associated with chromosomal abnormality. This condition did not hinder our love for her and the care we gave her had given us so many rewards as she had exceeded expectations of her cognitive abilities, had developed into a very cheeky, happy and loving child. We could have grieved for the loss of what we had expected, a normal, healthy child, but when true love exists no matter what imperfections; we realize we are capable of unconditional love. Being in a position to love and have a living, responsive child to be the recipient of that love brings happiness beyond any limitation. Now with Mary Jo's absence, we have extended this love to help other disadvantaged orphans, widows and others who are asking for help. We look forward to further extending our help to others, perhaps creating a foundation later to help children with special needs.

Our experience of grief and loss made us realize that grieving is something we will have until the end of our days.

This kind of grieving however is no longer pathologically destructive. During the early days of grieving, our mourning had consumed our hopes for a better future but now we know that although the sadness, the painful memories of her death process, the beautiful memories when she was still alive are very much a part of our existence, they will continue to occupy our mind from time to time, and sadness will never totally be erased from our hearts and minds, hope for the future has re-emerged.

We know our behaviour has changed, we reach out to people who are grieving and we are not afraid to be triggered by the emotions they feel. The pain of grieving cannot be dusted under the carpet or hidden and denied, it has to be experienced and felt and more important for grief to make us more committed to living our lives to the full, for one thing is certain no one lives forever.

Messages of Love for Mary Jo

Mary Jo Touched not only her parents' lives but many others also. This chapter records some of these beautiful memories.

~*~

Poem from Julie, Mary Jo's favourite child carer:

April 1996

MARY JO

You came to us in February

You look so very small

With smiling face and sparkling eyes

You soon stood very tall.

A Kiss From An Angel

Your Mother and Father loved you

We knew from the very first day

As they found it hard to leave you

And then to go away

Even for a short time

They always wanted to stay.

You ate and drunk, you smiled and cried

You brought us lots of joy

You loved to play every day with Sydney

Your favourite toy.

You listened to stories and danced and sang

To Janet Jackson's Theme

While Twinkle, Twinkle Little Star was

Always in your dreams.

Karate was your favourite sport

A sidekick you did with ease

While riding on your motor bike

Messages of Love for Mary Jo

To you was just a breeze.

Remember how upset we were

When you first began to sneeze

In addition, when you smiled your cheeky grin

Our hearts you always pleased.

And when you entered the Hospital

We farewell you in the car

How were we to ever know?

You were to become a 'Little Star'

You left in such a hurry

Some did not even get to say 'Goodbye"

And when we heard about you

We all began to cry

Oh, 'Mary Jo'

We will,

Always remember you

As you shine from your Cloud above

Because down here at Kanga's House

We know

Only 'Little Angels' bring such love

Love always from 'the Clouds'

~*~

Letter from Auntie Bebing: 20 October 2014

Hello little angel,

I am your aunt Raquel from America, the only surviving sister of your dad and the

Best friend of your Mom way back in the Philippines. Regretfully, we have never met. I wish I could tell you how I feel about you or reminisce about the moments we had together, but there's none. Sorry baby, it broke my heart that I missed what our friends and relatives had experienced in their interaction with you. Wish I had the chance to say that I loved you. Some say, you touched their lives when you came and had changed their lives when you left. They learn a lesson that there was no regret on the part of your parents when tragedy struck because they never delegated your care to anyone else but to themselves.

If alive, you will now be 21 years old on November 23, 2014. You must have wondered how Dad and Mom met. Well, Auntie Bebing did the matchmaking. I arranged that your mom pick up your dad from the airport when your Dad visited Philippines from Australia. The two met oblivious of my plan. I never wanted anyone other than my close friend, your Mom to be my sister in law and to challenge my brother, your Dad on his strong conviction not to remarry after being divorced for 10 years

Not too long after their meeting love sparked. For all I know your Mom had migrated to Australia. When you came into their lives, I have heard that you are a very cute, happy and cheeky little Angel, always smiling and had showed extra ordinary intelligence.

Auntie Bebing and Uncle Uwe Karl felt that we have a baby in you too, because we don't have any. We received pictures of you looking so pretty from the dirndl dresses (German dress)

Sent by Uncle Uwe. Then more cute pictures of you came but our favourite is the one where you are dressed in a karate kimono throwing kicks in the air. You took your style from your black belter Daddy. After 2 years and 4 months of those blissful days, we received devastating news that you had left us. I immediately arranged to fly to Australia to comfort your Dad and but

Unfortunately, my flight arrived on midnight of the day you are put to rest.

Again, I missed a very important chance to see you the last time. When your Dad and Mom picked me up past midnight, I saw them so sad, tired and devastated. At your small apartment, I saw your toys, clothing, pictures, cribs and everything about you and the pain in your parents' faces. You are amazing, my little Mary Jo. You made me aware that you are around us. That you were welcoming Auntie Bebing. That evening I slept in the bed so near to your crib with your doll lying on your pillow. Next morning, your mom frantically asked me if I rearranged the position of the doll in the crib. I was wondering why it was so important if it was rearranged. It was in a kneeling position, arms holding the crib railing and looking facing where I slept the night before. Did you watch Auntie Bebing while she was sleeping Mary Jo?

In the evening, on our way to church with your parent's friends, I suddenly hear a humpty dumpty song from one of the toys at the back compartment of the van. I was seated at the back. Everyone turned around and asked if I activated the toys. (Thinking to myself, what is so important with the toys activating. Why make a fuss? It turned out, you have the same toys as your friends and you always play music.

Did you do that my baby girl to make Auntie Bebing aware that you were especially with me? I realized, that I should not linger on the thought that I lost the chance of not knowing you but to be thankful that I was able to experience the moment in your household how life was when you were alive. Having said this, on the first morning after I arrived your Mom summoned me to be with her to say goodbye together to your Dad. That was his first day to go back to work after the tragedy. I learned that every morning you were the one handing the car key from the wall to your dad and I can picture you kissing Dad goodbye, Dad kissed you and Mom goodbye. Now, you are not there. With head bowed Dad took the key from Mom and kissed us goodbye.

Then I was ushered by Mom to your little apartment balcony to wave goodbye to Dad after backing up the car. No more Mary Jo to wave goodbye so AuntieBebing took over. Mom explained that she needed me that moment to ease the pain on the first day that you should be there in order to continue the rituals of daily life. Where you there watching us baby?

One time, after mass I saw your Dad as he walked down the stairs beside the church so sad and head bowed. Mom explained that he missed not having you on his shoulder after mass, which he had been doing

Messages of Love for Mary Jo

for the past 2 years and 4 months. Mary Jo, you are the first the last and the only angel your parents had. Your birthdays are always celebrated every year, attended by the same friends who love you so much. I wish I also had my very own Angel in heaven like my brother and my sister in-law. They are very lucky indeed.

Thank you little angel, Mary Jo for coming into our lives. You taught us the meaning of love. As the saying goes, "better to have loved and lost than not to have loved at all"

We miss you so much.

Love, Aunt Bebing and Uncle Uwe

~*~

Message from Uncle Mike: October, 2014

Beautiful memories never fade and sometimes as I search my treasure trove of happy and sad memories, the one labeled Mary Jo stands out among the rest. We all know that being touched by an angel is a life changing moment; likewise knowing that the angel is not physically present anymore could wreck your heart to pieces or simply bring a smile. Hoping for the moment one day to meet that little angel again, I go on with life amid the storm or sunshine. Until now, my mind refuses to accept that Mary Jo passed away. So tough to emotionally accept her absence. As I am writing now I tend to focus on the good things that came to me because of Mary Jo. I had come to really believe that Heaven exists because I physically saw an angel. My mind now tinkers on the noble beauty of people who have Down's Syndrome and are speedily aborted in America and other rich counties. Now that Down's syndrome can be easily diagnosed while the baby is still in the womb, millions of mothers had decided to kill the fetus in their womb. Only so called normal babies are allowed to live. A normal baby has the complete structure of DNA, which makes them highly intelligent and physically beautiful, but then the capacity to greed and power is there too. Can you name a Hitler or Genghis Khan with Down Syndrome? When I think of Mary Jo, I am encouraged to travel the road less traveled. To see beauty with the eyes of the heart, to plan and do things without the motive of profit and gains, to truly be human and seek my real reason for existence as well as open my arms to the so-called unwanted deformed people. By the way, who is dented and ugly anyway? I have my good answer now. Thank you so much Mary Jo for leading your uncle Mike to the real beauty of life. Forever I will be grateful. I miss you, I really miss you.

Uncle Mike

~*~

From Uncle Peter: October 2014

Heztilee, Jane and me opened your Facebook page and saw the draft cover of your book for Mary Jo. I had been having vision of a young girl in flowing white gown but the face wasn't so clear. Now I realized the vision must be Mary Jo as she is no longer a baby but a young lady now.

~*~

From Auntie Muffet: October 2014

I can very well recall that when we first slept in your bedroom when we visited you in Sydney, we felt so at home immediately. I was seeing Mary Jo's photo and had this massive feeling she was there in the room welcoming us.

From Uncle Joey: 30, August 1996

I know you both miss Mary Jo so much, but you likewise know that from now on until the next life you have a very powerful intercessor that will always be with you every moment of your lives. No word can describe your loss, but likewise, no word can describe the exalted glory where she is right now. Mary Jo showed us all that physical disability is no disability, that life is measured not by how long you lived but by how much you lived in it. Mary Jo' earthly life was short but she lived it to the full. Not many mortals have accomplished the same. What more can we ask?

From Paula (Director of Child Care)

Messages of Love for Mary Jo

~*~

My heart goes out to you both at this time of such grief and despair. The loss of one's child is like falling into the blackest hole that no light can ever penetrate again and the pain is unbearable. I remember the Padre's words about the quality of life being so important and not necessarily the length of one's life. That helped a little in the knowledge that Mary Jo's 2 years and 4 months was filled with love.

Mary Jo was such a happy joyful child, so eager to learn new things and enjoy the people that came into her life. She was also blessed by being given to you both. I will always remember that the deep bond of love you all have for each other and the dedication in making sure that Mary Jo had everything she needed.

Mary Jo accomplished so much in the short time she was here; she reached out and touched people's hearts just like you both do.

~*~

12 September 2014:

From Uncle Peter Mindoro Island, Philippines

Hello Mary Jo,

It's been quite a while, at least 20 years ago, since you came with your parents to visit us here in the Philippines. You were just a cute little girl, not of talking age yet, so we never had the chance to talk. We also didn't get to know each other well since there were so many of us trying to get your attention. So many uncles, aunties, cousins were competing for your attention at the same time. You were a tiny star and we were your big fans. That was the last time I saw you. Many memories of your few days of vacation have faded, buried under heaps of time and darkened by the tragedy of your passing away.

Yesterday, as the sun was coming down behind the ridges of the distant mountains, I prayed for the angels to help me dig back those faded memories and bring back to life the past, which I hardly had the chance to grasp. I knelt for quite a while at the high terrace of our unfinished home. I stayed still, occasionally saying a prayer for you, until darkness came. A thought came to me that you must be there in heaven already and that I should pray to get you there. So, I paused and waited for my mind to quiet down. Meanwhile, a cool soft breeze came and pushed away the lingering heat from the sun that had just gone down. I felt encouraged to continue my meditation while enjoying the soft onset of night. I prayed once more as a feeling of emptiness came upon me. It was as if I was not able to be really an uncle to you.

Something was missing between you and me. Something was lost so long ago. Knowing that there is nothing more that could be done to recover or make up for that loss made my feeling somehow painful but sweet. Painful because of the loss, but sweetness came along with it because the pain was telling me that the loss is meaningful and that my heart still beats for the pain of emptiness comes from the wound in the bond that still holds you close to me. At one moment, the twenty years that passed did somewhat vanish and my mind made a picture of you close to me. You surprised me, though. I thought I will see the little girl again, but oh, yes, you are now a young woman! Twenty years was just yesterday. This morning your little cousin Heztilee laughed at me. I told her that somehow I could hear you in my mind. (Yes, she knows all her cousins, uncles and aunties even though we live so far away and that she seldom meets them.) What made her laugh was because I suddenly cried as I was telling her that I could hear you. Embarrassing, but luckily no one else saw me cry.

When I was an administrator and finance officer of a school, I was criticized for continuing the operation of a department for handicapped children. (There were all sorts of handicaps –hearing-impaired, poor vision, missing limbs and many others including yours – the Down syndrome.) There were two official reasons for keeping SPED. First, it was a venue of practicum for our school's education department. Second, as a mission school, owned and operated by missionaries, it was part of our mandate to continue the education-related efforts of the priests and brothers who were there before us. For me, there was one reason I did not tell anyone – I love the kids. I was happy that they could go to school, especially in our school.

Looking back, I saw greed as a worse handicap than what you and other children were having. I also saw that having SPED in the campus makes our environment complete. Normal life means that there are always handicaps of different manifestations that we have to embrace. Erasing portions of reality that we don't like will not solve our problems. On the contrary, it will add more blind spots to our vision and thus creating for ourselves a self-induced handicap without realizing it. Looking back deeper, when I would visit SPED children in their place in school, I saw you in them. And with you being a part of me, I felt belonging to them. Loving them was just natural. I could only wish that you were there with us.

Your loving Uncle Peter

You must have read this letter in my mind even before I wrote it. Therefore, there's no need to send it to you. Besides, I don't know how. Instead, I will email this to your Mom and Dad.

~*~

16 October 2014: From Godmother Elnora

To our dear Mary Jo

Like your mum and dad I was excited when I first saw you almost 21 years ago. You were diagnosed with Down Syndrome but we still consider you a blessing from heaven. It was not an easy ride though for you and for me. I almost passed out when I saw your foot came out first. Your Apgar score was also low. That was your first fight to live and you fought it hard. You grew up to be a cute cuddly little girl. Always a smile on your face and gave a trusting hug to those around you. Your mum and dad were never tired searching for group support to give you the best of care. So many plans, so many dreams but life indeed is a roller coaster. The worst happened when you developed pneumonia. Again, you fought your hard fight but at such a young age, you were taken from us. We were devastated but it never equaled the pain your parents had. I grieved but probably I had a different mechanism of coping. Initially I cried but after that, I did not want to talk about it. I did not want to linger on the thought that you were gone. I refused to cry openly. Who will show me that karate kick? Who will give me that wet smacking kiss like you? Who will give me that cheeky look then smile? It took me a while to accept that you were no longer with us. Rest assured though, you touched us through our dreams that you were in a place of never- ending happiness. You became our angel and always there for us. So, I guess Mary Jo that was not goodbye. You were just ahead of us. For now, I will just be contented to feel your kiss and hopefully in time we will see you in heaven.

With much love, Ninang Nora.

~*~

From Elizabeth 19 April 1996

.....They love her so much. She is a very lucky little girl to have such parents. I say "have" and not "had" because Joe and Lulu speak about Mary Jo in the present tense. Lulu and Joe still have a little girl, and they always will; she just doesn't live with them anymore. Now, she lives with someone else. Last night, I saw so many photographs of Mary Jo that I feel I know her too. I have never seen a more photographed child! And in all those hundreds of pictures, what I saw was a beautiful little girl smiling, laughing, dancing, and kissing someone (usually her Dad). It was evident to me that Mary Jo was not only a much loved little girl, but that she gave back as much love.

~*~

Messages of Love for Mary Jo

From an anonymous card, an anonymous Poem: April 1996

For Such a Little While

God gave you your daughter

For such a little while

He put a bit of heaven

In the sunshine of her smile.

He took dust from the brightest twinkling stars

And made her sparkling eyes,

And now, she's gone back home to God,

To play up in the skies.

And though she left so quickly

That your hearts are grieved and sad,

We know she lives with God

And her small heart is glad.

And though your precious darling

Was just a rosebud small,

A Kiss From An Angel

She'll bloom in all her beauty

On the other side of the wall.

Anonymous Author

About the Author

Lourdes Villena Amoloria

We shall draw from the heart of suffering itself the means of inspiration and survival. **Winston Churchill**

~*~

Lourdes was born in Bacolod City, Philippines and is the eldest of nine siblings, seven brothers and one sister.

She migrated to Australia in 1991 where she met and went on to marry her loving husband Joe.

After trying for several years to have a child, Lourdes at the age of 40, finally received her gift from heaven. A beautiful much wanted and loved daughter who they went on to call Mary Jo.

Prior to her marriage, Lourdes had a very successful corporate career in sales and marketing with a multinational pharmaceutical and nutritional company. Her highest award was winning the

Philippines' Most Outstanding District Manager Award in the Pharmaceutical Industry.

Lourdes, after much soul searching, left her job to follow her heart's calling in Sydney, Australia.

KISS FROM AN ANGEL, is her masterpiece in showcasing how love, forgiveness and commitment to living, can facilitate recovery from the very destructive and unbearable pattern of emotions, behaviour, cognitive phase, physical and mental conditions that often follows after a significant loss.

It is her personal objective to help others understand their loss with as much compassion and humanness for the griever and their families. To assist others to gradually develop the mindset of assuming responsibility for their own recovery, using their own unique individualized ways of handling grief, at their own pace.

Her goal is to empower others to live an inspired and productive life even in their darkest hours of grief and loss. Lourdes believes that every person in your life is

About the Author

a gift from heaven, no matter how long his or her time on earth may be. If through the pages of this book she can help just one person overcome their grief and focus on the beautiful memories that their loved ones have left as their gift, then this book will have accomplished its purpose.

Lourdes is a degree holder in Bachelor of Arts major in Mass Communications.

She recently finished her Postgraduate in Counselling and is a Certified Life Coach.

Lourdes and her husband Joe live in Sydney and are committed to helping others through their grief so that they can move on with their lives as their loved ones would have wished for them to do.

Lourdes can be contacted via email:
lourdesvillenaamoloria@gmail.com or

Vial the mailing address:
PO Box 188 KINGSFORD NSW Australia 2032.
http://kissfromanangel.info/

"The best and most beautiful things in the world cannot be seen or even touched.
They must be felt from the heart".

Helen Keller

A loving Poem From My Mother

My mother's poem that always inspires me

~*~

Brighten the corner where you are

We cannot all be famous,
or be listed in the who's who,

But every person great or small,
has important work to do;

For seldom do we realize the importance
of small deeds,

Or to what degree of greatness,
unnoticed kindness leads;

For it is not the big celebrity
in a world of fame and praise,

But it is doing unpretentiously
in undistinguished ways;

The work that God assigned to us,

Unimportant as it seems;

That makes our task outstanding,

And brings reality to dreams;

A Kiss From An Angel

So do not sit and idly wish,

For wider, new dimensions;

Where you can put in practice,

Your many good intentions;

But at the spot God placed you,

begin at once to do;

Little things to brighten up,

The lives surrounding you;

For if everybody brightened up,

The spot on which they are standing;

By being more considerate,

and a little less demanding;

This dark old world would very soon,

Eclipse the Evening Star;

If everybody brightened up,

The corner where you are.

Salvacion Makilan Ruiz Villena

ISBN: 9780994188519

www.ingramcontent.com/pod-product-compliance
Lightning Source LLC
Chambersburg PA
CBHW072043290426
44110CB00014B/1565